D. C. (Daniel Clement) Colesworthy, John Tileston

John Tileston's school

Boston, 1778-1789 : 1761-1766 also, his diary from 1761 to 1766

D. C. (Daniel Clement) Colesworthy, John Tileston

John Tileston's school
Boston, 1778-1789 : 1761-1766 also, his diary from 1761 to 1766

ISBN/EAN: 9783337016258

Printed in Europe, USA, Canada, Australia, Japan

Cover: Foto ©ninafisch / pixelio.de

More available books at **www.hansebooks.com**

John Tileston's School.

Boston, 1778–1789 : 1761–1766.

Also, his Diary from 1761 to 1766.

By D. C. COLESWORTHY.

"What now appear to be only trifles, in after years will become important facts." — WILLIAM GOOLD.

BOSTON:
ANTIQUARIAN BOOK STORE.
1887.

TO

WILLIAM BLAKE TRASK,

A MODEST, UNASSUMING CITIZEN, A COURTEOUS,
CHRISTIAN GENTLEMAN,
WHOSE PERSEVERING RESEARCHES AND UNWEARIED LABORS IN THE
ANTIQUARIAN FIELD HAVE BEEN A SOURCE OF PLEASURE
AND PROFIT TO THE SONS AND DAUGHTERS
OF THE PURITANS, ·
OUR EXCELLENT FRIEND FOR MORE THAN A THIRD OF A CENTURY,
THIS LITTLE WORK IS RESPECTFULLY AND GRATE-
FULLY DEDICATED.

INTRODUCTION.

The people of New England owe a large debt of gratitude to her noble army of faithful and efficient teachers — many of whom, to instruct themselves and their children, have labored through a long series of years in patience and with perseverance, receiving in many instances but few words of encouragement, and a meager remuneration.

As a concise introduction to the account of one who labored probably longer than any other individual in his vocation in New England, I have given a chapter on the early schools of Boston. One cannot fail to notice the great improvement that has been made in the mode of teaching during the past two centuries, and the excellent facilities now afforded for the cultivation of the mind and the elevation of the affections. Undoubtedly the schools of New England, and especially the schools of Boston, come the nearest to perfection of any in this country or the world. The most capable teachers are secured, whilst no narrow policy warps the judgment of our committees, prompting them to withhold any reasonable amount of money that can be judiciously expended in the advancement of the cause of education, or in the moral improvement of the rising generation.

I have added short sketches of a few New England teachers who spent a large portion of their lives in preparing our children and youth for lives of prosperity and usefulness, whose names deserve to be held in grateful and perpetual remembrance.

INDEX.

Adams, John, 34.
Adams, Mr., 39.
Allen, Mr., 73.
Appleton, John, 27.
Atlantic and St. Lawrence Railroad Company, 24.

Bagley, John, 24.
Baker, 47.
Ballard, 74.
Barret, Deacon, 79.
Barret, Samuel, 76, 77.
Beckett, Sylvester B., 27.
Bingham, Caleb, 37, 39.
Blanchard, Caleb, 76.
Boroughs, Capt., 78.
Boston, 19, 38, 41, 43, 47.
Bostonians, 39, 40, 48.
Boston Latin School, 30.
Bowen, Penuel, 78.
Boyd, 47.
Bradford, Mass., 31.
Bright, Mrs., 68.

Burrill, Susan, 32.
Buxton, Me., 25.
Byfield Parish, 22.

Capen, 47.
Carter, Mr., 39, 79.
Carter, Nathaniel H., 23.
Cartwright, Capt., 74.
Central Church, 21.
Charlestown, 19.
Chase, Aquila, 31.
Chase, Caleb, 24, 31.
Chase, Wm. D., 32.
Cheever, Ezekiel, 19.
Cheever, Ira, 21.
Checkley, Mr., 77, 78.
Chelsea, 21.
Chester, N. H., 31.
Chichester, N. H., 28.
Clark, Daniel, 25.
Cobbitt, 47.
Coffin, C., 73.
Coffin, Charles, 34.
Coffin, Eliza, 73.

INDEX.

Coffin, Lydia, 34.
Coffin, Mary Barrett, 34.
Cogswell, William, 24.
Colesworthy, D. C., 27.
Colesworthy, Daniel P., 42, 47.
Collins, 47.
Commencement, 41.
Coney, Daniel, 69.
Contribution money, 80.
Cotton Hill, 14.
Crowell's lot, 14.
Cummings, Alex., 75.
Cummings, Sumner, 24.
Cushman, Bezaleel, 23.
Cutter, Edward F., 24.
Cutter, William, 25.

Darracott, William, 75.
Dartmouth College, 31.
Day of fasting, 72.
De Cheserau, 74.
Dere Island, 13.
Diary from 1761 to 1766–71.
Dickey, Capt., 77.
Dorchester, 16, 33.
Doubt, Dr. Nyott, 76.
Doubt, Mrs., 78.
Dow, Neal, 24.

Draper, Mr., 74.
Dummer Academy, 22.
Duren, Charles, 26.
Duren, E. F., 26.
Dwight, Wm. T., 32.

Early Schools in Boston, 13.
Eell, Sarah, 68.
Election, 41.
Eliot school-house, 17.
Empress of Russia, 71.
English grammar, 40.
Europe, 24.
Evening school, 71.
Everett, Edward, 36, 45.
Exchange street, 43.
Exeter, N. H., 23.

Faneuil Hall, 44.
Field, Mary, 36.
First Parish Church, 25.
Fowles, Rebekah, 33.
Fox, Edward, 26, 27.

Gardner, Francis, 30.
Genealogical Register, 24.
Governor and Council, 43.
Granary burial ground, 35.
Grant, Anna, 79.

INDEX.

Greenleaf, Stephen, 75, 76.

Haines, Edward P., 27.
Hamlin, Cyrus, 29.
Hampton, N. H., 31.
Harrod, Benj., 68.
Harvard College, 22, 30.
Hebron, Me., 23.
Hicks, Hezekiah, 15.
Hicks, Zachariah, 34.
High School, Portland, 25.
High Street Church, 29.
Holbrook, Abia, 16.
Holmes, Nathaniel, 68.
Holyoke, Samuel, 16.
Howard, Joseph, 25.
Hutchinsons, 17.
Hutchinson, Edward, 14.
Hutchinson, Thomas, 14.

Illsley, Silas, 26.
Independence, 41.
Ingersoll, Elizabeth, 68.
Ingraham, 47.
Ipswich, 19.

Jackson, Henry, 28.
Jackson, Timothy, 69.

Jenkin, Capt., 76.
Jewett, Jedediah, 27, 29.

Kendall, Amos, 23.
King of Spain, 72.
King, Rufus, 22.

Langdon, Mr., 79.
Laughton, John, 79.
Leach, Mrs., 77.
Leache, Mr., 75, 79.
Leverett, T., 78.
Libby, Joseph, 25.
Lloyd, Dr., 77.
Longfellow, Henry W., 24.
Longfellow, Stephen, 22, 24.
Lothrop, Ellen, 21.
Lovell, John, 16.
Lovell, James, 16.
Love, Susan, 14.

Maine, 47.
Maine Congregational Conference, 26.
Malcom, Mr., 78.
Marblehead, 21.
Martinico, 72.
Massachusetts, 33.

INDEX.

Massachusetts Charitable Society, 36.
Mather, Cotton, 20.
Merrill, James, 27.
Middlebury College, 29.
Moncton, Gen., 72.
Motley, John Lothrop, 30.
Moody, Franklin C., 27.
Moody, Samuel, 22.
Morrison, John H., 30.
Mountfort, 47.

Neats, Samuel, 79.
New England, 14, 19, 21, 30, 34, 37.
New Haven, 19.
New North Church, 80.
New York, 32.
North Bennet Street, 17.
North Grammar School, 16.
North School, 15.
North Writing School, 15, 34, 37.

Old South Church, 43.
Old State House, 43.

Page, Thaddeus, 36.

Parents and guardians of private scholars, 68.
Parker, Joel, 24.
Parsons, Theophilus, 22.
Patten, Stephen, 38.
Payson, Edward, 26.
Perkins, Jn'o, 72.
Phillips Academy, 31.
Phillips, Wendell, 30.
Pittman, 47.
Portland, 25, 28, 29, 31, 47.
Portland Academy, 24.
Portmorte, Philemon, 13.
Portsmouth, 28, 31.
Preble, Edward, 22, 24.
Prince, Mr., 71.
Prince, Hugh, 32.
Prince Street, 35.
Proctor, John, 15, 16.
Proctor, Master, 75.
Prophecies, 20.

Queen Street School, 15.

Roxbury, 43.

Salem, 21.
Saltonstall, Mary, 68.

INDEX.

Scholars from 1761 to 1765, 49.
Scholars from 1778 to 1789, 55.
Shattuck, George C., 30.
Shaw, Jason, 26.
Shepley, Ether, 24.
Shippard, William, 68.
Shurtleff, Roswell, 31.
Shurtleff, Nathaniel B., 30.
Sigourney, Capt., 72.
Smith, 47.
Smith, Henry B., 26.
Southack, Capt., 15.
South Boston, 16.
South End, 42.
Southgate, Horatio, 26.
South Grammar School, 16.
South Writing School, 15, 16.
Stackpole, Charles A., 26, 27.
State of Maine, 47.
Stevens, Mad'm, 73.
Strong, Caleb, 22.
Stuart, the celebrated, 44.
Symonds, Mr., 74.

Tansur singers, 74.
Third Parish Church, 26, 32.
Thomas, Elias, Jr., 79.
Thomson, Mr., 20.
Tileston, Hannah, 33.
Tileston, John, 16.
Tileston, Timothy, 33.
Tucker, Phil., 69.

Vernon, Capt., 74, 75.
Vermont, 26.
Vinal, John, 16.

Wainwright, Mr., 14.
Walpole, N. H., 30.
Washington, George, 41, 42.
Washington Street, 42.
Waterville College, 26.
Webber, Mr., 79.
Webb, Mr., 76.
Webb, Nathan, 36.
Webb, Sophia, 36.
Whitmore, Maj.-Gen., 71.
Willard, President, 22.
Williams, 47.

INDEX.

Will, Mr., 74.
Winslow, Albert, 32.
Wiswall, Peleg, 16.

Writing School, Queen Street, 16.

York, Me., 22.

EARLY SCHOOLS IN BOSTON.

THE first settlers of Boston, as soon as they opened a house for public worship, commenced looking after the education of their children. As early as April 13, 1634, at a meeting called by the inhabitants of the town, "it was gen'ally agreed upon, that our brother, Philemon Portmorte, shall be entreated to become schoole-master for the teaching and nourtering children with us."

January 10, 1642, "Dere Island" was ordered to be improved for the maintenance of a Free School for the Town.

In the year 1647 a law was enacted, by the General Court held in Boston, for the establishment of Public Schools throughout the province. One reason given by our wise fathers for the education of the young was, that "Satan" had a "strong hold of ignorance," and the establishment of schools and general instruction would tend to counteract the influence of that "ould deluder." This legislative enactment was undoubtedly the first law of a similar import in New England.

In March, 1652, the town provided for the enlargement of the "skoole house."

March, 1696, it was voted in town-meeting to build a house for a writing school at Cotton Hill, "adjoining the ould schoole house."

In 1717, a school-house was located upon the Common, "adjoining to Crowell's lott, over against Mr. Wainwright's."

March 11, 1718, at a town meeting, Thomas and Edward Hutchinson offered to build a school-house at their own expense, for a free writing school at the north part of the town, and it was voted that part of the land bought of Mrs. Susan Love be taken for that purpose.

At a town meeting, September 28, 1720, a committee was appointed "to consider about erecting a spinning school for the

EARLY SCHOOLS IN BOSTON.

instruction of the children in town," and the committee recommended the building of a house for this purpose "in the waste land before Captain Southack's."

In 1739 there were five public schools in Boston, in which nearly 600 pupils were taught. In the South School there were 120 scholars; in the North School, 60; in the North Writing School, 280; in Queen Street School, 73; in the South Writing School, 62. In May, 1749, the number of scholars had increased to 705, and in 1757 to 741.

In 1743, Zachariah Hicks, usher in John Proctor's writing school, who had a salary of 150 pounds, petitioned for an increase of pay, and 30 pounds were added.

The committee, appointed by the selectmen to visit the public schools in March, 1758, was accompanied by the representatives of the town, overseers of the poor, and by several clergymen and physicians. They reported that the "Schools were all in good order." They found in the North Writing School 220 scholars; in the

North Grammar School, 36; in the South Writing School, 240; in the South Grammar School, 115; in the Writing School in Queen Street, 230. Total, 841 scholars.

At this period there were also several private schools taught in town.

In 1764, the town voted to pay the following sums to the teachers: John Tileston, of the North Grammar School, 100 pounds; Peleg Wiswall, of the same school, 100 pounds; Abia Holbrook, of the Writing School on the Common, 100 pounds, and John Vinal, his assistant, 50 pounds; John Lovell, of the South School, 120 pounds; and James Lovell 60 pounds, and John Vinal 50 pounds, ushers in the same school; John Proctor, of the Writing School in Queen Street, 100 pounds, and Samuel Holyoke, of the same school, 80 pounds.

By a legislative act in 1804, when a portion of Dorchester, now South Boston, was annexed to Boston, it was stipulated that the proprietors of the land, among other assignments, should set apart a lot on which a school-house should be erected, at some future period.

The school-house, where Mr. Tileston taught, was a small building on North Bennet Street, where the Eliot schoolhouse now stands. This is the lot given to the town by the Hutchinsons.

From the commencement of the present century the Boston schools have continued to improve, so that now they are equal, if not superior, to any schools in the country. The best educated and most conscientious teachers are employed, and no small amount of money is yearly expended in various channels by efficient committees, to secure important results. Whatever has a tendency to advance the pupils and elevate the schools, is made available in every possible direction. It is questionable if in any large city of the Union as much rigid care is observed to educate the young and to prepare them for the varied duties of life. The schools of Boston are distinguished as model institutions, and the youth who are trained in them, being thoroughly prepared for any department in science or trade, find no difficulty in securing desirable positions; the fact of their graduation being a guarantee of their fitness, and the best recommendation they could offer. Many of our successful merchants, our statesmen, philosophers, and clergymen, have graduated from the Boston schools, and are now exerting a wide and salutary influence, not only in New England, but wherever civilization and religion have a dominance. That our schools may continue to flourish and send forth streams to elevate and bless our common country and the world at large, should be the prayer of every moralist and every Christian.

EARLY TEACHERS.

EZEKIEL CHEEVER.

EZEKIEL CHEEVER was born in London, January 25, 1614, and in 1637, at the age of twenty-three years, he came to New England, landing in Boston. In the fall of the same year we find him in New Haven, where, in 1638, he commenced teaching a public school, and where he continued his labors for about a dozen years. In 1650 Mr. Cheever removed to Ipswich, Massachusetts, taking charge of a free school. After teaching eleven years in this place, and making his school "famous in all the country," he removed to Charlestown, Massachusetts, in 1661, to take charge of a free town school that had been established in the place. After laboring nine years in Charlestown, he removed to Boston, January 6, 1670, where, notwithstanding his age, he continued to teach the " Free Schoole " for a period of thirty-eight years. When he took charge of this school " it was agreed and ordered," by the committee, " that Ezechiell Cheevers should be installed in the free schoole as head master thereof: likewise that Mr. Thomson should be invited to be an assistant to Mr. Cheevers in his worke in the schoole." It was also agreed "that the said Mr. Cheevers should be allowed sixty pounds p. an. for his service in the schoole, out of the towne rates, and the possession and use of ye schoole house."

Mr. Cheever was the author of one or two school books and a volume of three short essays on the Prophecies. He died August 21, 1708, aged ninety-four years, after having taught school for seventy years. Cotton Mather preached a sermon on the death of Mr. Cheever, a copy of which lies before me. " He Dy'd, Longing for Death," the good Doctor remarks.

At the close of his sermon, Mr. Mather gives a quaint poem entitled,

EARLY TEACHERS.

GRATITUDINIS ERGO.

The master was

"Praised and Lov'd of Well-instructed Youth,"

and,

"All the *Eight parts of Speech* he taught to them,
They now Employ to *Trumpet* his esteem."

To "proclaim to Posterity" the worth of so excellent a man, we are told that

"Ink is too vile a Liquor; *Liquid Gold*
Should fill the Pen, by which such things are told."

Mr. Cheever was twice married. His first wife, a New Haven woman, died in 1649. His second wife, Ellen Lothrop, of Salem, died in 1706. He left several children whose posterity are numerous throughout New England. The late Ira Cheever, deacon of the Central Church in Chelsea, Massachusetts, and for many years a teacher in Salem, Marblehead, and Boston, was a descendant of Master Cheever.

SAMUEL MOODY.

Samuel Moody, for thirty years Preceptor of Dummer Academy at Newbury, Byfield Parish, Massachusetts, was born in York, Maine, in 1725; and was a son of Rev. Joseph Moody. He graduated at Harvard College in 1746, and taught school in his native town until he was called to take charge of the Academy. Mr. Moody was a thorough Greek and Latin scholar, and prepared for college many a student who became celebrated in after life. Among his pupils in York and Newbury were President Willard, of Harvard; Caleb Strong, Governor of Massachusetts; Edward Preble, the distinguished Commodore; Judge Stephen Longfellow, grandfather of the poet; Theophilus Parsons, and Rufus King.

Mr. Moody was a remarkably faithful instructor, and labored indefatigably to impress upon the minds of his scholars their duties to each other and to their Creator. He was exemplary in the discharge of every duty, and prompt in all his engagements. He died in Exeter, New Hampshire, December 14, 1795, aged seventy years.

BEZALEEL CUSHMAN.

BEZALEEL CUSHMAN, a native of Hebron, Maine, was born September 14, 1785. His father was one of the first settlers of the town. Naturally a studious boy, at the age of sixteen years he had acquired a good knowledge of the common rudiments of education, and was thought competent to teach a district school, which he did to the satisfaction of the committee; but feeling the need of a more thorough education, he prepared himself for college, and entered Dartmouth, supporting himself by teaching during his vacations. Mr. Cushman graduated in 1811, in a class, several of whom became celebrated. Among others, Amos Kendall, Postmaster-General; Nathaniel H. Carter, whose letters from Europe, several years ago, attracted no little attention, and which in 1825 were published in two octavo volumes; Caleb Chase, for several years a teacher in Portland and other places; William Cogswell, D. D., first editor of the *Genedlogical Register;* Chief-Justice Joel Parker and Ether Shepley, LL.D.

In 1815 Mr. Cushman took charge of the Portland Academy, and for twenty-six years continued in the faithful performance of his duties. Among his pupils were Stephen Longfellow, Jr., Henry W. Longfellow, Edward Cutter, Edward Preble, Sumner Cummings, Neal Dow, and our venerable friend, John Bagley, of Portland. The latter two only are living.

In 1841 Mr. Cushman relinquished his duties as teacher, and obtained through the influence of his former pupils, a situation as Surveyor of the Port of Portland, which position he retained for the space of ten years. He was subsequently clerk of the Atlantic and St. Lawrence Railroad Company.

A conscientious, upright, Christian gentleman, for a long period Mr. Cushman was one of the deacons of the First Parish Church in Portland. He died June 21, 1857, aged seventy-one years and nine months.

JOSEPH LIBBY.

JOSEPH LIBBY was born in Buxton, Maine, December 13, 1793. He learned the trade of a blacksmith, but seriously injuring himself while at work, he was not able to continue his laborious employment, and commenced a course of study preparatory to a collegiate education. He entered Bowdoin, and graduated in 1821, in the class which contained among others William Cutter, Daniel Clark and Joseph Howard.

Soon after leaving college Mr. Libby was chosen principal of the High School in Portland, which had just been established, where he continued a faithful and efficient teacher for nearly thirty years, preparing scores of young men for entering college, and for various duties in life. The writer was one of his pupils in 1824. Among our school-mates at this period were Bishop Horatio Southgate; Edward Payson, son of the distinguished divine, and the author of several entertaining works; Charles A. Stackpole, an able writer and ready speaker; Rev. Silas Ilsley, a Baptist clergyman; Professor Henry B. Smith, a distinguished theologian; Deacon E. F. Duren, the indefatigable scribe of the Maine Congregational Conference; Judge Edward Fox, one of the ablest lawyers that Maine has produced; Charles Duren, now settled over a Congregational church in Vermont; Jason Shaw, who entered Waterville College and died while an undergraduate; and several others who have been more or less distinguished.

For more than a third of a century Mr. Libby was a deacon in the Third Parish Church, and for as long a period he was superintendent of the Sabbath-school connected with the parish. Always ready to speak in public, he took an active part in the conference meetings, and his seat was seldom vacant.

In 1850 Mr. Libby resigned his position as principal of the high school; at which time a large number of his former pupils assembled, and made arrangements for a public meeting, to present to their faithful teacher some memorial of their respect and love.

A committee was chosen for this purpose, consisting of the following: Jedediah Jewett, Charles A. Stackpole, Edward Fox, John Appleton, D. C. Colesworthy, Edward P. Haines, Franklin C. Moody, Sylvester B. Beckett, and James Merrill; all of whom, with the exception of Charles A. Stackpole and the writer, after a period of thirty-five years, have passed away.

Accordingly in August the old pupils convened and presented to Mr. Libby a beautiful silver pitcher. John Appleton, then a member of Congress, made an appropriate address, which was happily responded to by Mr. Libby. It was an interesting occasion to all concerned.

Mr. Libby died August 27, 1871, aged seventy-seven years.

HENRY JACKSON.

HENRY JACKSON was born in Chichester, New Hampshire, August 1, 1783. For several years he taught school in various towns in his native State, until 1811, when he was called to teach in Portsmouth. There he remained, faithful in the discharge of his duties, until 1824, when the school committee of Portland induced him to remove to that town and take charge of one of the principal schools in the place. He continued his labors for the space of twenty-six years, when in 1850, on the 22d day of August, he died at the age of sixty-seven years.

In the winter of 1828 Mr. Jackson taught an evening school for young tradesmen and apprentices, where we had the pleasure of being numbered among his pupils. Cyrus Hamlin, LL.D., the distinguished missionary, and now President of Middlebury College, was also one of the scholars. On one occasion Mr. Jackson gave out the subject of profane swearing as an essay for the pupils to write upon. A committee was appointed to decide to whom the prize should be awarded, and it fell to Cyrus Hamlin.

Mr. Jackson for several years was a member of the Third Parish Church. At the formation of the High Street Church in 1831, he was set off with the writer and several others, to help form the new society, where he continued an active and useful member until the day of his death.

Kind, genial, and intelligent, Mr. Jackson secured the love and affection, not only of his pupils, but of scores of friends who sadly grieved when he departed. Mr. Jackson was the author of an arithmetic that was used for many years in the schools of Portland.

His old pupils have erected over the remains of Mr. Jackson a substantial monument as a token of their respect for his memory.

FRANCIS GARDNER.

FRANCIS GARDNER was born in Walpole, New Hampshire, March 15, 1812, and graduated at Harvard College in 1831, in the class with Nathaniel B. Shurtleff, John Lothrop Motley, George C. Shattuck, Wendell Phillips, John H. Morrison, and other men of distinction. Soon after leaving college he took charge of the Boston Latin School, where he remained a devoted and efficient instructor until his death — a period of more than forty years. Mr. Gardner probably fitted more pupils for college than any other teacher in New England.

In 1843 Mr. Gardner with great labor prepared a dictionary of the Latin language, which has been extensively used in Boston and other places.

Mr. Gardner died January 10, 1876, aged nearly sixty-four years.

CALEB CHASE.

CALEB CHASE was born in Chester, New Hampshire, February 4, 1783. He was a descendant of Aquila Chase, who emigrated to this country and settled in Hampton, New Hampshire, in 1640. Mr. Chase fitted for college at Phillips Academy, Andover, and in 1807 entered Dartmouth College. While an undergraduate he connected himself with the Congregational church, under the care of Rev. Roswell Shurtleff. Graduating in 1811, he commenced teaching in Bradford, Massachusetts. In 1817 we find him in Portsmouth, New Hampshire, where he taught the principal school in the place for two or three years. In 1820 Mr. Chase removed to Portland, Maine, and took charge of the center Grammar School, as successor to Mr. Hugh Prince. The school-house was on Back Street, now Congress Street, opposite the Third Parish Church. The building was burnt in the great fire of July 4, 1866, which destroyed nearly one third of the city. Mr. Chase, whose health was impaired, relinquished his charge and was succeeded by Mr. Albert Winslow.

After Mr. Chase gave up teaching, for a season he kept a grocery store in Portland, and died September 20, 1850, aged sixty-seven years and seven months. The services at his funeral were conducted by his pastor, the late Rev. Wm. T. Dwight, D.D.

Mr. Chase married Susan Burrill, who died in 1856. He left several children. William Dwight Chase, of Brooklyn, New York, is the youngest son of Mr. Chase.

JOHN TILESTON.

AMONG the early settlers of New England we frequently find the name of Tileston. John, son of Timothy and Hannah Tileston, who was born in Dorchester, Massachusetts, in 1701, was the father of John Tileston, who married Rebekah Fowles, January 21, 1730. These were the parents of JOHN TILESTON, who was born in Boston, February 27, 1735. When John was an infant, he was severely burnt by falling into the fire, and the consequence was so serious an injury to one of his hands that the complete use of his fingers he never recovered. He was thus incapacitated for mechanical or other employments that required the full use of his hands. Notwithstanding this affliction the defective hand became perfectly adapted to the holding of a pen and for writing. After leaving school, at the age of fourteen, young Tileston was placed under the care of Zachariah Hicks, master of the North Writing School, in Boston, where he served faithfully an apprenticeship of six or seven years. A portion of this period Mr. Tileston was a school-mate of John Adams, the second President of the United States, who through a long and busy life tenderly remembered his early friend. They both died the same year.

At the age of twenty-five, October 23, 1760, Mr. Tileston was married to Lydia Coffin, daughter of Charles and Mary Barrett Coffin.

In 1762 Master Hicks resigned his position, and Mr. Tileston was elected principal instructor in the school, which position he retained, to the satisfaction of several committees, until he reached the advanced age of eighty-five years, when in 1819, feeling the infirmities of years increasing, with the decay of strength, natural to so long and laborious a life, he found it necessary to resign and retire from his active duties.

As Mr. Tileston had devoted more than seventy years to instructing the young, the committee were induced to continue his salary as long as he lived. His death occurred on Friday, October 13, 1826, when he had nearly completed his ninety-second year, and after a happy married life of sixty-six years. Services at his funeral were held at his late residence, No. 65, Prince Street, on Saturday, where many of his fellow-citizens and his old pupils collected to pay their respects to one greatly beloved. His body was interred in the Granary burial ground. His wife, Lydia, survived him four or five years, and died May 21, 1831, aged ninety-five years. Provision had been made by the proper authorities to continue a salary sufficient for the support of Mrs. Tileston during her life.

Mr. Tileston's will is dated March 5, 1814. He left to his wife the property he possessed. The witnesses to the will were Nathan Webb, Mary Field, and Thaddeus Page.

Mrs. Tileston's will is dated October 20, 1827. According to the schedule her property amounted to $5,233.67, which she left to a nephew and four nieces, with a portion to Sophia Webb.

Although Mr. Tileston was not wealthy, he had frequent opportunities, which he cheerfully improved, of bestowing charities liberally on the unfortunate and destitute. Sympathizing with the poor and distressed, he was one of the original projectors of the Massachusetts Charitable Society, which was one of the first benevolent institutions in the Commonwealth. He invariably attended the meetings of its members, which comprised many of the most respected and influential citizens of Boston.

The late Hon. Edward Everett, who was a pupil of Mr. Tileston, and who was intimate with him as long as he lived, once remarked: "The only murmurs I ever knew him to utter were when he could do no more good; yet as fast as he had the ability, he poured the oil and the wine upon such as stood in need of assistance."

Mr. Tileston was a strict disciplinarian, and his reproofs were administered with impartiality, and his punishments with rare judgment, as I have heard my father, who was one of his pupils, often remark. He never left in the minds of his scholars a feeling of disgust or rancor. They respected and loved him, even when he was administering the severest reproofs.

Mr. Tileston's chirography was very uniform and neat, as I have noticed in the copy books in my possession, left by my father. The copies were written by the master, and the scholars endeavored to imitate them. I have seen the handwriting of many of Mr. Tileston's pupils, who generally were excellent penmen. Mr. Caleb Bingham, author of the *American Preceptor* and the *Columbian Orator*, who was for many years an usher in the North Writing School, under Mr. Tileston, wrote also a beautiful hand. I have before me a letter from Mr. Bingham to my old friend, the late Stephen Patten, of Portland, who was for a season an instructor in the school, which is a fine specimen of pencraft. As a portion of the letter relates to the school, I give an extract. It is dated Boston, August 29, 1792: "I know you will participate in my joy, when I inform you that I have gained a complete victory over my school-boys. They are now nearly as still in the school as the girls. I was obliged to relinquish my method of detaining them after school, on account of Mr. C.'s conduct. I resolved then to bring the matter to a crisis, and know whether I was master or not. I laid aside all books for the day and spent it in preaching. The next day I undertook to find what virtue there was in the old *maple whig of seventy-six*.[1] I belabored them from day to day, till they finally gave me the victory. Now and then an old woman, and a few who are

---

[1] This was a large ferule which had been used in the school for many years.

not worthy the name of *men*, and who oppose the doctrines of our *forefathers*, have murmured, and complained to the committee. But the boys are *silent* in school, and that is the main object with us; and I hope we shall be able to *silence* their parents. A certain Mr. Adams, whom we used to hear from last winter, came into the school this day with a complaint against the usher, and told us that he would not allow of his boys' receiving corporal punishment on any occasion whatever. We shall, therefore, expel them for the next offence."

The good penmanship, for which Bostonians have always been famous, is due in a great measure to the labors of Mr. Tileston and his assistants, Mr. Bingham, Mr. Carter, and others. The merchants, mechanics, and even the laborers of Boston, eighty, ninety, and a hundred years ago, who were taught in Mr. Tileston's school, seemed to be particularly uniform and correct in their penmanship. A glance at old letters, day-books and journals of this period, is convincing proof of the thoroughness with which the pupils were drilled.

Previous to 1789 there were few if any of the public schools in Boston where English grammar and some other branches of education were thoroughly taught, and so it fell to the lot of the master of the writing school to teach spelling, reading, and grammar, and Mr. Tileston was equal to the task. To this portion of his duties Mr. Tileston gave particular attention. He devoted several hours each day, from which nothing diverted him, to the training of his pupils. In early life I noticed that the Bostonians, who were taught in Mr. Tileston's school, were excellent readers and generally correct in their spelling, and seemed well fitted for almost any position in life. So much for the judicious and persevering labors of a faithful and devoted teacher, who was a thorough disciplinarian and sincerely loved his employment.

Afternoons, when school was not kept, Mr. Tileston usually employed his hours of relaxation, when the weather was favorable, in fishing in the harbor, or in riding through the neighboring towns. Frequently he took extended walks, accompanied by some of his friends, which he seemed particularly to enjoy. He was often associated with two or three of his former pupils, who esteemed it a perfect treat to walk or ride beside the "Master," as he was familiarly called, so dearly cherished and tenderly beloved. The anecdotes and reminiscences of former pupils, and of earlier days, which he rehearsed, afforded much diversion to them all. On Commencement, Election, and Independence days, he usually visited among his friends abroad, where he was cordially received and bountifully entertained.

When his old pupils visited Boston, after a long absence, it gave him rare pleasure to invite them to his house, where he amply repaid them for their former kindnesses.

October 24, 1789, was a proud day for Boston, and for Mr. Tileston in particular. The illustrious personage, George Washington, was to visit the place, and extensive preparations were made by the town authorities to receive him. And the no little interesting part of the programme was the appearance of the school children in town, neatly dressed, with quills in their hands, full of smiles and radiant with delight. My father, Daniel P. Colesworthy, who died in Portland, in 1852, was one of Mr. Tileston's pupils at this period. At my request he wrote an interesting account of the occurrence which follows:

"When General' Washington visited Boston I was a school-boy. The day before he arrived Master Tileston told all the boys to come to school the next morning with clean faces, and dressed in their best clothes; each one to be particular to bring a quill with him. We followed our master's instructions, and accordingly the next morning we marched with the scholars belonging to the other schools in town; our school taking the precedence, and the South End school following in the rear. We marched to Washington Street, as far as the upper corner of Exchange Street, where we halted — opened to the right and left and formed a line on each side of the street, from Exchange Street to the Old South Church. At about half past ten o'clock the cannon on the Neck announced Washington crossing the line between Boston and Roxbury. The companies of militia of Boston and vicinity were out to escort him. A stage or bridge was built from the Old State House to the stores on the opposite side of the street, with arches underneath. It was covered with damask. Here the Governor and Council received him. An anthem was sung, as Washington, with his hat in his hand, passed by us on his light gray horse. We rolled our quills between our hands, that the General might notice us. When school was dismissed we called to see him, each one making a bow, which he politely returned. I saw him several times afterwards."

Mr. Tileston, being an unobtrusive man, never expressed himself in a positive or dictatorial spirit. He was social and kind to the most humble, and delighted especially to converse with little children. He was indeed a friend to the poor and unfortunate, and all classes felt perfect freedom in his presence. He had no children of his own, and so he seemed to be the parent of his whole school; looking after them, advising with them, and leading them in paths of virtue and happiness. And so for years his memory was cherished by his pupils, till one and another yielded to the divine mandate and passed away, to rejoin their master, as we trust, in a better world.

The following is a proof of the little esteem in which Mr. Tileston held himself. Several of his former pupils proposed to raise a sufficient sum of money to secure a full length portrait of himself, to be painted by the celebrated Stuart, and after it was finished to place it in Faneuil Hall, or in some other public place, but he would not consent. Finally, after much persuasion, he reluctantly yielded to the earnest desires of his friends. Thinking seriously over the matter, and feeling that no former school-master had been thus honored, he prevailed upon the gentlemen to relinquish their design.

In speaking of Mr. Tileston, Edward Everett remarks: " Master Tileston was a writing-master of the old school. He set the copies himself, and taught that beautiful old Boston handwriting, which, if I do not mistake, has in the march of innovation (which is not always the same thing as improvement) been changed very little for the better. Master Tileston was advanced in years, and had found a qualification for his calling as a writing-master in what might have seemed, at first, to threaten to be an obstruction. The fingers of his right hand had been contracted and stiffened in early life by a burn, but were fixed in just the position to hold a pen and a penknife, and nothing else. As they were also considerably indurated, they served as a convenient instrument of discipline. A copy badly written, or a blotted page, was sometimes visited with an infliction which would have done no discredit to the beak of a bald eagle. His long, deep desk was a perfect curiosity shop of confiscated balls, tops, penknives, marbles, and jewsharps, the accumulation of forty years. I desire, however, to speak of him with gratitude; for he put me on the track of an acquisition which has been extremely useful to me in after life — that of a plain, legible hand."

Hundreds have remembered Mr. Tileston with the same grateful feelings. There are but few living who attended his school. I know of but two or three, and it was at a period when Mr. Tileston was so infirm that he did little except to superintend the school, leaving the care of the pupils to his ushers. The descendants of his scholars are scattered all over New England, and, indeed, they may be found in nearly every State in the Union.

It is a matter of regret that we have not a complete list of the names of Mr. Tileston's scholars, which number many thousands during a period of more than seventy years, but when he taught in colonial times, and in the early days of the republic, as much care was not taken as at the present period to keep a perfect record. The first list comprises the names of those who attended his school from 1761 to 1765, and the second from 1778 to 1789. We have no list of the scholars from 1766 to 1777; a period of eight or nine years. Neither have we a record of those who were his pupils beyond the year 1789. If there were records kept we have not been able to find them. However, what we have given will, I doubt not, interest the descendants of Mr. Tileston's scholars, whereever they may have taken up their abode.

At the commencement of the present century, several of his old pupils removed to Portland, as business was comparatively dull in Boston; inducements being held out by the merchants of this thriving town, in the district of Maine. Among others we may mention the names of Baker, Boyd, Capen, Cobbit, Colesworthy, Collins,

Ingraham, Mountfort, Pittman, Smith, and Williams. Others went further east, and their posterity are numerous in the State of Maine.

The diary of Mr. Tileston is a meager one; but we have extracted from it every line that would be likely to interest the children of old Bostonians, and the descendants of his pupils.

SCHOLARS

WHO ATTENDED JOHN TILESTON'S SCHOOL
FROM 1761 TO 1765.

Adams, Abraham
Adams, Benjamin
Allen, John
Andrews, John
Archibald, Edward
Atkins, Charles
Atkins, Henry
Atkins, Nathaniel
Atkins, Silas
Audebart, Josiah
Audebart, Philip
Ayers, Henry
Badger, Abel
Badger, Stephen
Baker, John
Ballard, Benjamin
Barber, George

Barber, Nathaniel
Barnett, Samuel
Barns, Thomas
Barrett, Samuel
Bass, Joseph
Bass, Philip
Bazin, Thomas
Bell, Daniel
Bell, William
Bennet, Michael
Bennet, William
Bicner, William
Bill, John
Biordan, Thomas
Blasdell, Ephraim
Blasdell, John
Blunt, John

Blunt, Ezekiel
Bouve, Gibbon Sharp
Brazer, Edward
Breck, Daniel
Bright, John
Brickford, Alexander
Brown, Ephraim
Brown, Gawen
Brown, John
Brown, Joseph
Brown, Joseph L.
Burbeck, Henry
Burt, James
Butler, David
Butler, Ephraim
Butler, Gilliam
Butler, Samuel
Carter, William
Cathcart, John
Cartwright, Thomas
Cartwright, Timothy
Cary, James
Cary, Samuel
Cazneau, Joseph
Chadwell, Benjamin

Checkley, John
Checkley, John W.
Checkley, Samuel
Cheever, Bartholomew
Clark, Joseph
Clark, Samuel
Clough, Goodwill
Clough, John
Coffin, Charles
Colesworthy, Newcomb
Condy, Thomas
Connell, James
Coolidge, Benjamin
Coolidge, John
Coppinger, Stephen
Cross, John
Cross, Joseph
Cross, William
Cullern, David
Cumber, John
Cunningham, Thos.
Darracott, David
Darracott, William

SCHOLARS. 51

Davis, Solomon
Dickey, James
Dillehunt, William
Dinsmore, Archibald
Dobel, John
Dobel, Roleson
Dodge, Ebenezer
Dolbear, Benjamin
Doster, Andrew
Douglass, John
Eayers, Henry
Eddy, Joseph
Edes, Ebenezer
Edes, Jonathan
Eliot, John
Eliot, Samuel
Englis, Thomas
Eustes, Joseph
Farmer, Thomas
Foster, Edward
Francis, Archibald
Freeland, William
Gardner, John
Gardner, Thomas
Gibbons, Bouve
Goldthwait, Thomas
Gordon, William
Grandy, Joseph
Greenough, David
Greenough, Nathaniel
Greenough, William
Greenwood, Isaac
Griffith, John
Hammatt, Benjamin
Hammatt, Joseph
Hancock, Samuel
Harris, Samuel
Harris, William
Harrod, James
Harrod, Joseph
Hartt, Ralph
Hatch, Ezekiel
Hatch, Nolen
Hayden, Elkanah
Heligar, Peter
Hemmenway, ——
Hervey, John
Hill, Edward
Hill, John

Hill, Nathaniel
Hill, Samuel
Hitchborn, Samuel
Hobby, John
Holland, Christopher
Hopkins, John
Hooton, John
How, John
How, Joseph
Howard, Nathaniel
Howard, Samuel
Howland, Joseph
Hutchinson, William
Ingerfield, John
Inglish, Alexander
Inglish, Thomas
Inglish, John
James, Thomas
Jenkins, Benjamin
Jenkins, Jonathan
Jones, Benjamin
Jones, John
Jones, John Coffin
Kiddle, James
Lambert, Nicholas

Langdon, Ephraim
Langdon, William
Larrabee, Thomas
Leach, John
Lewis, Jonathan
Lewis, Philip
Lillie, John
Loring, John
Lymmes, William
Marchant, William
Marble, Thomas
Marrable, Thomas
Marston, John
Maverick, Samuel
Maverick, Jotham
Matthew, Fairservice
McArthur, William
McCleary, Robert
McCleary, William
McIntyre, Daniel
McIntyre, James
McIntyre, Robert
McLeod, Thomas
Milliken, James
Nazro, Isaac

SCHOLARS.

Newell, Benjamin
Newell, John
Nichols, William
Ogilvie, George
Orr, John
Page, Benjamin
Page, Jonathan
Paine, John
Patten, Nathaniel
Philips, John
Pierce, Hardy
Pigeon, John
Prevear, Edward
Prichard, Benjamin
Prince, John
Prince, Joseph
Prince, Thomas
Procter, E.
Procter, Samuel
Pulling, Joseph
Rand, Waffe
Raymant, Samuel
Rea, Nathan
Rea, Uriel
Richards, William
Richardson, Richard
Richardson, Thomas
Rickey, George
Riddle, James
Riddle, Thomas
Ridgeway, James
Ridgeway, Samuel
Ridgeway, Thomas
Ridon, Thomas
Robb, George
Robb, James
Robb, Thomas
Roberts, John
Roby, James
Roby, William
Ross, James
Ross, Matthew
Saltonstall, Leverett
Saunders, Robert
Shaw, Francis
Shaw, John
Shaw, Samuel
Shaw, Thomas
Shaw, William
Sheppard, Thomas

Sigourney, Andrew
Sigourney, Anthony
Sigourney, Charles
Sigourney, Elisha
Skillin, Simeon
Skillin, Solomon
Smith, John Kilby
Smith, William
Smith, William K.
Smith, Richard
Soper, Benjamin
Spear, Nathaniel
Stavers, Bartholomew
Stevens, John
Stevens, Wiswal
Stoddard, Thomas
Sweatser, Nathaniel
Symmes, William
Thayer, Cornelius
Thomas, James
Thomas, Jonathan
Townsend, David
Townsend, Thomas
Treat, Robert
Treat, Samuel
Trout, Thomas
Tudor, William
Turell, Joseph
Turner, Simeon
Vaughan, David
Vaughan, Nathaniel
Vaughan, William
Vernon, Thomas
Walker, Richard
Walsh, Jacob
Walsh, John
Webber, Richard
Webber, Seth
Wells, Francis
Wells, Samuel
Wendell, John P.
Whatley, Robert
White, John
Whiting, Joseph
Whitney, William
Whyte, James
Whyte, John
Widger, John
Willis, Charles

Willis, Nathaniel
Williston, Joseph
Williston, Josiah
Winter, Joshua
Woodman, Henry
Woolven, John
Wotton, James
York, John

SCHOLARS

WHO ATTENDED JOHN TILESTON'S SCHOOL FROM 1778 TO 1789.

Abrahams, Ralph
Abrams, Joseph
Adams, John
Adams, Joseph
Adams, Joseph N.
Adams, Kidder
Adams, Philip
Adams, Thomas
Adams, Thomas V.
Alesworth, Christopher
Alexander, Giles
Alexander, William
Alley, Nathaniel
Ames, Thomas
Andrews, Ebenezer
Andrews, Samuel
Andrews, William
Archer, Philip
Atten, Anthony
Austin, Ebenezer
Austin, Thomas
Avery, Benjamin
Baber, Nathaniel
Bachoon, Benjamin
Badger, Daniel

Badger, John
Badger, Joseph
Bailey, Joshua
Baird, James
Baird, John
Baird, Joseph
Ball, Isaac Towns
Ballard, Daniel
Ballard, John
Bangs, Edward
Barber, Joseph
Barber, William
Barker, John
Barker, William
Barnard, John
Barnard, Moses
Barnes, Benjamin B.
Barret, Jeremiah
Barret, Joshua
Barret, William
Barrett, Smith F.
Barross, William
Barton, Jonathan P.
Barton, William
Bass, Elisha
Bass, John
Bass, Moses
Bass, Philip
Basset, Edward
Baty, Gideon
Baxter, Paul
Bayley, John
Bennet, William
Bennett, John
Bentley, Samuel
Berry, Ebenezer
Berry, Thomas
Blair, Victor
Blasland, Thomas
Blasland, William
Booth, John
Booth, Jonathan
Bowland, John
Boyd, Ebenezer
Boyd, John
Boyd, William
Braden, Bartholo.
Bradley, David
Bradley, Moses
Bragdon, Nathaniel

SCHOLARS. 57

Breck, Joseph
Breck, Samuel
Breed, John C.
Brown, Nathaniel
Brown, William
Browne, Gibbins
Browne, John
Bruton, John
Buckminster, David
Bulfinch, Samuel
Bullmore, John
Burdit, James White
Burstead, Benjamin
Butler, Anthony
Butler, James
Cabbot, Joseph
Cades, Samuel
Callender, Ebenezer
Callender, John
Campbell, John
Capen, Edward
Capen, Stoddard
Capen, Thomas
Car, Benjamin
Carder, Richard
Carey, Edward
Carey, William
Carlton, William
Carpenter, Samuel
Casneau, William
Caswell, Samuel
Chadwick, Joseph
Chamberlane, Thos.
Chamberlane, Edw.
Champney, Caleb D.
Champney, Joseph
Chandler, Ebenezer
Chandler, John
Chandler, John T.
Chandler, Joseph
Cheeseman, John
Cheeseman, Samuel
Christy, James
Christy, Roland
Clark, Benjamin
Clark, John
Clark, Jonas
Clark, Joseph
Clark, Nathaniel
Clark, Samuel

Clark, William.
Cleary, Robert
Clive, Philip George
Clough, John F.
Clough, Joseph
Clough, William
Cobbit, Charles
Cobbit, John
Cobbit, Thomas
Cobbit, William
Cole, Charles
Cole, Elisha
Cole, Jacob
Cole, Samuel
Cole, Willam
Colesworthy, Dan'l P.
Colesworthy, Nath'l
Collins, Clement
Collins, John
Colpran, James
Conner, John
Cook, James
Coome, Ezekiel
Cooper, John
Cooper, Samuel
Cornell, Cornelius
Coverly, John
Craft, Edward
Cross, Thomas
Cunningham, Wm.
Curnber, John
Curtis, Benjamin
Cushing, Damon
Custain, Ezra
Dakin, Joseph
Daly, John
Darricot, William
Davies, Joshua
Davis, Elisha
Davis, John
Davis, Joseph
Davis, Nathaniel
Davis, Robert
Davis, Samuel
Dawes, Edward
De Cartevet, John
Devens, Richard
Dillaway, Thomas
Dinsdell, John
Doak, John

SCHOLARS.

Doak, William
Dodd, George
Dodge, Samuel
Dodge, Unite
Dodge, William
Dolbeare, Benjamin
Downes, Isaac
Downes, Shubael
Downes, Simeon
Drummond, Andrew
Drummond, George
Dunnell, Samuel
Dyer, Joseph
Dyer, William
Edes, Edward
Edes, Thomas
Edwards, Abraham
Edwards, Alexander
Edwards, Richard
Eliot, Samuel
Ellingwood, Ralph
Emmes, Clark
Emmes, Henry
Emmons, Aaron
Emmons, Henry
Emmons, Joshua
Emmons, William
Fairservice, Robert
Fanning, James
Fanning, Thomas
Farnham, Henry
Farnham, Newark
Farrey, John
Farrey, William
Fellows, Jonathan
Felts, Richard
Fenley, Robert
Fenno, William
Fitzgerald, Thomas
Flagg, Benjamin
Floyd, Richard
Folts, George
Folts, William
Fosdick, Phineas
Foster, John
Foster, Moses Brown
Freeland, John
Freeman, Isaac
Freeman, Thomas
Gardner, William

Garrett, Joseph
Gallop, Benjamin
Gallop, Richard
Givin, Nathan
Gleason, Benjamin
Godfrey, Moses
Goldthwait, Benj.
Goldthwait, John
Goodridge, James T.
Goodridge, John
Goodridge, Sam'l W.
Grabb, Samuel
Grant, James
Greenleaf, Oliver C.
Green, John Brown
Green, Richard
Green, Robert
Greenough, David
Greenough, John
Greenough, William
Groom, Richard
Hagger, Benjamin
Haley, Charles
Haley, Daniel
Hall, Edward
Hall, Jacob
Hall, Timothy
Hallen, Christian
Hallet, Job
Hallowell, Samuel
Hallowell, William
Haman, Casper
Haman, Edward
Harding, Isaac
Harris, Isaac
Harris, Leach
Harris, Samuel
Harris, Stephen
Harris, Nathaniel
Harris, William
Harrison, William
Hartt, Edward
Hartwell, John
Haskell, Mark
Haskins, Richard
Hatty, Michael
Hayden, Joseph
Hayden, Samuel
Hausst, Joseph
Hayter, Stephen

SCHOLARS. 61

Heath, Andrew
Heath, E.
Heath, Samuel
Heath, Thomas
Heath, William
Heffron, Jeremiah
Hemmenway, David
Hemmenway, Ebe'r
Hemmenway, Israel
Hemmenway, Joseph
Hemmenway, Peter
Hemmenway, Sam'l
Henley, Charles
Henley, James
Herdand, Nathaniel
Hewes, Nathaniel P.
Heyler, William
Higginson, John
Hiller, John M.
Hillman, Robert
Hills, Elias
Hills, John
Hills, Samuel
Hitchborn, Barret
Hitchborn, Benjamin
Hitchborn, John
Hitchborn, Nathan'l
Hitchborn, Philip
Hitchborn, Samuel
Hodges, Charles
Hodges, Leonard
Holland, Thomas
Homer, Andrew
Homer, Samuel
Homer, William
Hopkins, David
Hopkins, Henry
Hopkins, Nathaniel
Horne, Joshua
Hotty, Joseph
House, Edward
Howard, Samuel
Howe, Nathaniel
Howe, Robert
Howe, Thomas
Hudson, William
Hunt, John
Hunt, Joseph
Hunt, Samuel
Hyler, William

Ingalls, Benjamin
Ingalls, Robert
Ingalls, Stephen
Ingerfield, Paul
Ingerfield, Peter
Ingerfield, Thomp'n
Ingersoll, Abraham
Ingersoll, John
Ingraham, Nathaniel
Ingraham, William
Jackson, Daniel
Jackson, George
Jackson, Henry
Jackson, John
Jarvis, Benjamin
Jarvis, John
Jarvis, Samuel
Jenkins, Joseph
Jenkins, Samuel
Jenkins, William
Jenks, Henry G.
Jenks, William
Jennison, John
Jennison, John L.
Jennison, Samuel

Jones, James
Kemble, Thomas
Kennedy, William
Kent, John
Kettell, Thomas
Kidder, Abraham
Kidder, Joseph
Kirkwood, James
Kissick, Francis W.
Knox, Barnabas
Knox, Robert
Kuddock, Samuel
Kust, Enoch
Laka, Samuel
Lamb, Samuel
Lambert, George
Lambert, John
Lambert, Thomas
Lambert, William
Langley, Daniel
Larkin, Freeman R.
Larkin, Samuel
Lask, Robert
Laughton, Dan'l W.
Lawrence, Joshua

SCHOLARS. 63

Lawrence, Thomas
Leach, Melineuse
Lewis, Amos
Lewis, George
Lewis, James
Lewis, John
Lewis, Thomas
Lilley, Henry
Lillie, John S.
Lillie, Jonathan
Lillie, Thomas
Linn, James
Litchie, Thomas
Lombard, James
Lombard, Thomas
Lord, Alexander
Lord, John
Lord, Robert
Lord, Samuel
Lord, William
Loring, David
Loring, Edward
Loring, Henry
Loring, Joseph
Loring, Thomas

Loring, William
Lothrop, John
Low, Cornelius
Luckins, Thomas M.
Luckis, Benjamin
Magean, Moses
Makins, Samuel
Malborn, Godfrey
Mansfield, Amos
Marten, Abiel
Martin, John
Marstin, Nathaniel
Mason, Samson
Matchett, William
McCarty, Charles
McClarey, William
Mooris, Joseph
Meers, Daniel
Meers, Nehemiah
Meisories, William
Meisories, Joseph
Mellage, James
Mellage, John
Milldollar, Philip
Mills, James

Minns, Henry
Minns, Thomas
Mitchell, John
Moody, William
Moore, Thomas
Morgan, John
Morris, Thomas
Morse, Samuel
Moseley, David
Mountfort, Joseph
Neat, John
Newcomb, William
Newman, John
Newman, Joseph
Newman, Thomas
Newman, Timothy
Noble, Arthur
Noble, James
Noble, John
Norton, Elisha
Norton, Richard
Oliver, Benjamin
Oliver, Ebenezer
Oliver, Joseph
Oliver, William Pitt

Owen, Benjamin
Page, Benjamin .
Palmer, Andrew
Palmer, Francis
Palmer, Samuel
Parkman, Samuel
Peak, John
Peak, Ralph H.
Pendexter, Alex.
Penny, Henry
Perkins, John S.
Perkins, Samuel
Pierce, John Badger
Pierce, Jonathan
Pierce, Joseph
Pierce, Thomas
Pierce, William
Piermont, John
Piermont, Thomas
Pike, Benjamin
Pike, Enoch
Pike, Timothy
Pittman, Joshua
Polley, Jacob
Pook, Charles

SCHOLARS.

Presson, Nicholas
Prout, James
Pulsifer, David
Pulsifer, James
Ramsdell, David
Rand, Isaac
Rand, James
Rattey, William W.
Rayment, Edmund
Raymond, William
Rayner, John
Revere, Paul
Rhoades, Ebenezer
Rhoades, Isaac
Rhoades, Jacob
Rhoades, John
Rhoades, Stephen
Rice, Richard L.
Richards, John
Richardson, Jona.
Ridgeway, Philip
Riverley, William
Robbins, Francis
Robbins, James
Roberts, Benjamin
Roberts, John Tate
Roberts, Thomas
Roberts, William
Robinson, Benjamin
Robinson, Edward
Robinson, John
Rogers, Joseph
Rogers, Samuel
Rose, Philip
Ruddock, Edward
Ruddock, John
Salmon, John
Saunders, William
Savage, William
Seward, Benjamin
Seward, Thomas
Skelton, Stephen
Skelton, William
Sigourney, Anthony
Sigourney, Peter
Sinclair, Thomas
Singleton, Thomas
Skillen, John
Skillings, Neh. W.
Skinner, David

Skinner, Richard
Skinner, Simeon
Skimmer, William
Smith, Francis
Smith, Robert
Smith, Robert H.
Smith, William
Smithwick, Francis
Snelling, James
Snelling, John
Snelling, Joseph
Snow, Ambrose
Snow, Jeremiah
Snow, Thomas
Snow, Simeon
Spence, Peter
Starr, Joseph
Starr, William
Stevenson, Benj.
Stevenson, Thomas
Stillman, John
Stillman, Samuel
Stoddard, David
Stoddard, Seth
Stodder, Jonathan

Stone, Samuel
Swift, Benjamin
Symmes, John
Tate, Thomas Frail
Taylor, Benjamin
Tenneys, Richard
Thomas, Alexander
Thomas, George
Thomas, John
Thomas, Joseph
Thomas, Thomas K.
Thompson, David
Thompson, James
Tileston, John
Townsend, David
Townsend, Samuel
Tucker, John
Tucker, Samuel
Turner, William
Tyler, Edward
Tyler, Ellis
Vincent, George
Vincent, Joseph
Vincent, Thomas
Waine, Edward

Waine, Thomas B.
Waine, William
Walker, Ezekiel
Walker, John
Walker, Joshua
Walker, Newark J.
Walker, Thomas
Wallace, Samuel H.
Walls, Samuel
Walls, Thomas
Warner, Daniel
Waters, Samuel
Webb, Nathan
Webb, Thomas
Webb, William
Welch, William
Weld, Giles
Wells, Benjamin
White, Ebenezer
White, Samuel
Whitman, Edward
Williams, Edward
Williams, John
Williams, Thomas
Williston, Friend
Williston, John
Williston, Joseph
Woodward, William
Wyer, David
Wyer, John
Yandells, Samuel

PARENTS AND GUARDIANS

OF JOHN TILESTON'S PRIVATE SCHOLARS, 1761–62.

In 1761 and 1762 Mr. Tileston taught a private school for boys and girls, in connection with his public school, as I learn from his diary and his ledger. He kept a regular account with the parents and guardians of his pupils, whose names are given below. In his accounts with the parents and guardians I find that they were all charged with "Books, Pens and Ink." The price of tuition was three pounds a quarter.

Besides paying for their own sons and daughters, Nathaniel Holmes paid for Sarah Eell's schooling; Benjamin Harrod for Mary Saltonstall; Mrs. Bright for Elizabeth Ingersoll; William Shippard for

PARENTS AND GUARDIANS.

Phil. Tucker, and Daniel Coney for Timothy Jackson.

Adams, William
Allen, Widow Eliza.
Andrews, John
Atkins, Henry
Atkins, Silas
Badger, Abel
Bailey, James
Baker, Widow Mary
Baker, Nathaniel
Bass, Philip
Boucher, Thomas
Breck, Widow
Breed, Nathaniel
Bright, Mrs.
Brown, John
Brown, Jonathan
Butler, John
Butler, Mrs. Mary
Campbell, Mr. (tailor)
Carey, Jonathan
Carey, Richard
Checkley, Samuel
Cheever, William
Clemens, James
Clough, John
Clough, Joseph
Coney, Daniel
Crosby, Mrs. Mary
Dexter, Samuel
Dobel, John
Eliot, Andrew
Emmerson, Edward
Eustis, Joseph
Fairservice, James
Goldthwait, Thomas
Greenwood, Nath'l
Hammett, Benjamin
Hancock, Nathan
Harrod, Benjamin
Hill, Alexander
Hobby, Rev. Mr. (of Reading)
Holmes, Nathaniel
Horton, John

How, Joseph
Howland, Nathaniel
Hutchinson, Thos.
Jenkins, David
Jenkins, Jonathan
Jones, Ichabod
Lenox, David
Lewis, Philip
Loring, Nathaniel
Page, William
Paine, William
Parkman, Mrs.
Phillips, Richard
Prebble, Col.
Procter, Benjamin
Pulling, John
Rand, Nathaniel
Rea, Uriel
Robb, James
Ruddock, John
Russell, James
Savage, Samuel P.
Shaw, Francis
Shippard, William
Sigourney, Andrew
Skillin, Simeon
Snelling, Mary
Spear, Nathan
Stoddard, After
Stone, Thomas
Thomas, Elias
Thomas, James
Thomas, William
Townsend, Shippy
Tudor, John
Turell, Joseph
Wells, Francis
Wendell, Mrs. Han-
  [nah
White, John

DIARY OF JOHN TILESTON.

1761 to 1766.

1761. Sept'r 15. Had a new Hatt of Mr. Prince. Price £12.

Sept. 20. My old Hatt new lin'd.

Oct'r 12. Open'd Evening School.

Oct'r 24. Great wind.

Oct'r 26. Went to B—y. Gave M—r 5 Doll's. (Great storm.) Bot. 4 Cords Wood, cost £2. Bot. 10 Baskets Charcoal, £3 0s. 0d.

Nov. 4. Bo't 12 Baskets of Coal, £3 10s.

Dec. 6. Paid the Excise on Tea and Coffee.

Dec. 11. His Excellency Major General Whitmore was drowned.

1762. Jan. 5. Died, Elizabeth, Empress of Russia.

Declared war against Spain.

Jan'y 15. Window's Sash put up new, and fence painted and Cellar Doors; new Hearth; new Floor; new fence between Latin School.

Feb. 16. Martinico taken by the English; General Moncton, Commander.

April 14. Declar'd war (at Boston) against the King of Spain.

May 7. 137 Boys at School at one Time in the forenoon.

May 10. 139 Boys present at one Time.

May 17. 136 Boys present.

May 18. 140 Boys present.

May 19. 136 Boys present.

June 14. 158 Boys present at once (afternoon).

July 3. I had of Mr. Jn'o. Perkins, 2 Rheams of Paper; one at 5–10; the other at 4–10.

July 28 was observ'd as a Day of Fasting and Prayer throughout the Province, on account of the Scorching Drought.

July 30. We had a fine soaking rain, almost all day.

Aug. 1. 137 Boys present at school.

Aug. 23. 133 Boys present (exclusive of private scholars).

Aug. 27. Capt'n Sigourney sent me a Jugg of Rum.

Sept. 7. Began to take in Wood at School. 137 Boys present (exclusive of private scholars).

Sept. 7. Took the house of Mad'm Stevens, at £100 per annum. Lodg'd in it the 13th of September. (Graining.)

Sept. 7. 30 feet of Wood at School. 10 feet more Oct. 8.

Sept. 8. Bought a knife of Mr. S–g–d. Cost 20s. old ten.

Sept. 22. 6 feet do. at house.

Oct. 8. 12 feet do. at do.

Oct. 10. 36 feet do. at do.

Sept. 30. We had our roast beef frolic at hog Island.

Died the 30th Sept. Eliza. Coffin, Daughter to Brother C. Coffin, aged 7 years and 9 months.

Oct. 21. Mr. Allen gave me a present of £3 15s. old ten.

Oct. 29. Began to make Fire at School.

Began to take the Newspapers of Mr. Draper, at 50*s*. per annum. Paid 25*s*. in part thereof.

Nov. 4. Bot. of Mr. Symonds (our Milk Man) 4 Barrels of Cyder at 50*s*. old ten, per Barrel — £10.

Nov. 6. Tack put up.

Nov. 15. Bot. 6 Baskets of Coal for £1 16*s*.

Nov. 16. The Tansur Singers at my House.

1763. Jan. 13. Renew'd my Licence. Mr. Will and De Cheserau being my bondsmen.

Feb. 2. Bot. 4 Baskets of Coal for 20*s*.

March 23. Capt'n Vernon sent me a present — 2 doz'n of pickle Limes, Cocoa Nuts and other sort of Nuts.

Capt'n Cartwright sent me some pickle Limes (a pail full).

April 26. My Desk brought home.

May 11. 145 Boys present (exclusive of P. School).

Aug. 2. I had of Mr. Ballard 8 Cordwood for my House and Aug. 3 I had 6 Cord for School at £6 per Cord.

Aug. 4. Our frolick at Spectacle.

Aug. 9. Capt'n Vernon sent me 1-2 Dozen Oranges.

Aug. 9. The Singers at my House.

Aug. 10. Peace proclaimed at Boston. (Training Day.)

Thursday, 25th of Aug., died the Rev'd Mr. Alex'r Cummings, æ 37. His disorder was the billous Cholick.

Sept. 16. Mr. William Darracott took the Key of the Barn — he to give 5 Dollars per year as rent for the same.

Sept. 23. B–r–d of Mr. L–h £50 old ten, to pay Interest for the same till paid.

Sept. 26. Lent Master Proctor 1,000 quils. Oct. 10, lent 1,000 ditto. Dec. 27, lent Mr. Proctor 100 quils. Jan. 4, 2,000 ditto.

Oct. 22. I transplanted a Mulberry Tree of Mr. Leache's.

Oct. 22. Stephen Greenleaf came to my house.

1764. Feb. 23. Singers at my House.

Ap'l 9. Stephen Greenleaf came again after having the Small-pox.

I gave 3 pistoreens for my 6 Ovals.

Ingredients for 1 quart of Ink — 4 ounces of Galls of Aleppo, 2 ounces of Copperas, 2 ounces of Gum Arabic.

May 7. Capt'n Jenkin paid me and made an allowance of 20*s*. for keeping me so long out of my money.

June 7. Doct'r Nyott Doubt died.

Aug. 22. 147 Boys present, exclusive of private scholars.

Sept'r 15. I had a pair of gold buttons of Mr. Webb.

Oct'r 29. Paid Mr. Sam'l Barret £15.00. Old Ten's, it being what I gave towards building the new north Steeple.

I had a new Russel Gown.

1765. Feb'y 4. I had the following Reams of Paper of Mr. Caleb Blanchard, *viz*., 1 of £9; 1 of £6, 7, 6; 1 of £3, 15. Total £19 2*s*. 6*d*. Paid the 14th of Nov'r, 1765.

Feb'r 23. Bought a Hog which weigh'd 244 lbs. Cost £30 10s. 6d.

March 14. Bought 1 Ream of Paper at Deacon Barret's. Paid £5 0s. 0d.

March 30. Chimney swept and Bacon put up.

April 22. Chimney swept in the Kitchen.

Ap'l 1. Made 1 doz. Cyphering books with 10 1-2 sheets in each.

April 6. Being Sabbath day Capt'n Dickey's house caught on Fire in the morning, just before the second Bell rung, but was speedily extinguished. In the afternoon of the same day we were again alarmed by Mr. Checkley's house being on Fire, and it like to have prov'd a great Fire. Every thing was mov'd out of the House, and the top of the House was intirely broke open.

April 8. Mrs. Leach del'd of the 7th son, successively.

April 22. Apply'd to Doct'r Lloyd.

April 30. Mr. Bartlett sent me a Dozen of Bristol Beer.

April 30. Rev'd Mr. Penuel Bowen was Ordained to the Pastoral Care of the New South Church and Colleague with the Rev. Mr. Checkley. (We broke up school and went.)

May 18. Bought of Mr. Salter 8 Slates for 48s., and 100 pencils for 15s.

June 12. Had of Mr. T. Leverett 2 Rheams of Paper. (July had 2 quires blue paper.)

June 26. The Select Men visited the Schools.

Aug. 2d. Had two Cords of Wood of Mrs. Doubt, from Mr. Gable's Wharff, at £5 10s. per Cord.

Aug. 1. Made 6 doz. best books.

Aug. 8. Made 1 doz. Cyphering books, 10 1-2 sheets in each.

Aug't 21. Had of Mr. Malcom 12 Cord and 1-2 of Wood (6 1-2 at School), at £5 10s. per Cord.

Sept. 16. Bought of Capt'n Boroughs at the Town Dock ten thousand quills at 45s. per thousand. I likewise bought at the same place 4 thousand for Master Proctor.

Sept. 14. Mr. Elias Thomas, jun., bought Eleven Hundred Quills for me at 4s. per hund. Little after, Mr. Thomas bought two thousand four hundred more.

Oct. 10. Made 5 1-2 doz. books, best paper.

Nov. 14. I had a pair of double soled pumps of Mr. Webber, £3 10s.

Nov'r 21. Died, Master Langdon (of a fever) æ. 32 yrs.

Nov'r 27. Mr. Carter's Father died very suddenly.

Dec'r 26. Miss Anna Grant died of a Consumption.

1766. Jan'y 25. School Chimney altered. Cost £1 2s. 6d.

Sept. 4. I was a Bearer to Mr. John Laughton's wife.

Sept. 29. Bought a Ream of Paper at Deacon Barret's. Cost £6 15s.

Nov. 20. Mr. Samuel Neats died, greatly lamented by all who were acquainted with him, aged 44.

Among other matters the Diary contains the amount Mr. Tileston "put into the Contribution box" every Sabbath for several years, commencing 1763. The amounts vary from ten and three pence to nine shillings. The aggregate is a no trifling sum for a man in moderate circumstances.

There is also "An Account of Contribution Money for my Pew, since Jan'y 1st, 1768," to Dec., 1774. The sums vary from ten shillings to one, two, and three pounds. Mr. Tileston worshiped at the New North Church.

www.ingramcontent.com/pod-product-compliance
Lightning Source LLC
Chambersburg PA
CBHW020330090426
42735CB00009B/1480